THE STORY OF LIFE
6

Empires and Ideas
1750 ~ 1914

MICHAEL POLLARD

Illustrated by
ROBERT G. HUNTER

Blackie

Contents

Text © Michael Pollard 1981
Illustrations © Blackie & Son Ltd 1981

First published 1981
ISBN 0 216 90735 7
All Rights Reserved

BLACKIE & SON LTD
Bishopbriggs, Glasgow G64 2NZ
Furnival House, 14-18 High Holborn,
London WC1V 6BX

Printed in Great Britain by Cambus Litho, East Kilbride

1.
Years of change

This book takes the story of life in Britain from about 1750 to the beginning of our own century. In those 150 years, life changed for everyone far more quickly than it had done since the beginning of history.

In 1750 most people worked on the land, and farming gave Britain most of its wealth. By 1900 Britain had become a land of factories, and most people earned their living in them. In 1750 the only way to travel was on horseback, or in a cart or carriage pulled by horses. In 1900 there were still many thousands of horses in use, but trains, cars and buses were making travel easier for everyone. In 1750 any sea voyage was slow and dangerous, in a small sailing-ship. By 1900 steamships had conquered the oceans of the world. In 1750 most people in Britain lived in small villages. By 1900 millions had crowded into towns and cities.

If you were to travel back in time to 1750 you would find the world very strange. There were few schools, few hospitals, few doctors, no big shops, no proper roads and no proper postal service. Most of the things we take for granted today just weren't there. But if you were to travel back only as far as 1900, you would find things a bit old-fashioned, but in many ways quite like the world of today.

In 1750 Britain was beginning to build up her *Empire* [1]. The British had settled along the east coast of what is now the United States of America. There were British *settlements* [2] on the coasts of India and Africa. Although Britain lost her American colonies in the War of Independence in 1783, the rest of her Empire continued to grow until, by 1901, it covered about one quarter of the land surface of the earth. But other countries, too, wanted empires — and, as you will read in this book, this led to war. In the end, it led to the First World War of 1914 to 1918, the worst war the world had ever known.

Two other great changes were about to start in 1750. Historians call them the *agricultural revolution* and the *industrial revolution*. These are not very good names, because a revolution is usually something that happens quickly and is soon over. The agricultural and industrial changes that took place after 1750 were gradual and took a long time.

1

The British Empire about 1800 (shown in red)

The agricultural revolution meant better ways of rearing animals and growing crops, using machinery to do many of the jobs on the farm that had, up to then, been done by manpower. Machinery was costly to buy and keep in working order. It could "pay for itself" only if it was used as much as possible — and this meant that large fields and large farms made more profit than small ones. Using machines also meant that fewer people were needed to work on the land.

The industrial revolution was also about replacing manpower with machine-power. Fewer goods were made at home or in small workshops, and more in large factories employing hundreds of people. In the factories steam power was used to drive the machinery, and coal was needed to fuel the boilers that made the steam. So the industrial revolution led to more coal-mining. Factory-workers and miners had to live near their work, and so the new industrial towns and cities grew quickly in size.

For most people in Britain, all these changes brought more sadness and worry than happiness, and many of the stories in this book are sad ones. But when you have reached the end, you will be able to explain why the book is called *Empires and Ideas*.

2.
Ben Turner's land

My name is Ben Turner. I want to tell you what happened in our village of Littleton when the **squire** [3] and the big farmers took away our land.

It was in the year 1755. Up to then, most of the men in the village, like me, worked for the squire or one of the farmers and also had a little land of their own. There was a plot of land down by the river that had always belonged to my cottage. No one knew how long this had been so, and I didn't have any papers to prove it. But you ask anyone in Littleton — they'll tell you that Top Cottage had that plot of land down by the river.

I grew vegetables down there. My wife, Meg, and later on our sons, helped me with it. Some of the vegetables we kept for our own table, and some we sent to market. I'd go down there most days after work, and the time I spent there was worthwhile. Round our way, if anyone grows some particularly fine vegetables, people say, "they're as good as Ben Turner's."

It wasn't an easy life, but if you were ready to work hard and had a good wife like Meg you could live quite well. We brought up six children — four boys, two girls — in our house, and none of them ever went hungry.

Then, in 1755, everything changed.

The first thing I knew about it was when the squire's **agent**[4] came to see me. He wasn't polite about it, either. He didn't come to my house to talk business like a gentleman. No, he stopped me in the fields one day.

He reined up beside me on his horse and looked down at me.

"Turner," he said.

"That's my name," I said.

"That land of yours down by the river," he said. "Do you pay rent for it?"

"No," I said. "It goes with my cottage. Always has done."

"I'd like to see the papers about that," he said. "You have got papers to prove it, have you?"

He knew I hadn't, of course.

"The master's putting up a **Bill**[5] to Parliament to have the village land **enclosed**[6]," he said, "including your piece by the river."

"Enclosed?" I said. It was the first time I'd ever heard the word.

"It's no good trying to farm with little bits of land here and there," he explained. "Our new ploughs and **drills**[7] need room — bigger fields, better crops, more money for us all."

He dismounted. "That's why the master's going to tidy things up. He wants your land by the river, and several other people's too."

I was getting angry. "Why should I give up my land?" I said.

The agent tried to calm me down. "Oh, the master isn't just going to take it," he said. "In return, he'll let you have a plot about the same size on Chalk Hill."

"Chalk Hill?" I said. "Nothing grows up there, and everyone knows it. How am I going to dig it? It's like iron up there."

He shrugged his shoulders. "Well, there it is," he said. "I've no time to argue with you. I just came to warn you. Don't do any more to that land by the river, because it won't be yours much longer. Probably the master will be kind enough to let you gather the crops you've already planted. Good-day."

And with that he mounted and rode off.

When I got home that night I was shaking, partly with anger and partly because I couldn't see how Meg and I could live without our piece of land.

4   "Eat your supper and don't worry so," said Meg.

"There won't be many more suppers," I said, "if this Enclosure Bill goes ahead."

I went round to see my neighbour, Tom. He was as furious as I was, but he had seen enclosures before in another village and told me about them.

"If we want to complain," he said, "we'll need a lawyer to fight our case for us and that would cost money. And the lawyer will be a friend of the squire's anyway, so the squire will be sure to win."

"So we've just got to put up with it?"

"Yes, that's all we can do."

"What if we stop his men putting up fences round our land?"

"Then the master will send soldiers to sort us out."

Tom turned out to be right. The squire's friends in Parliament all voted for his Enclosure Bill. In place of my *fertile*[8] plot of land down by the river, I was given some of the stoniest ground on Chalk Hill. We tried working the land on Chalk Hill for a year or two, but you could see from the start that it was hopeless. It was too dry and stony. Some of the men gave up after one year. I went on for a bit longer, but it wasn't worth it. I was working for nothing. So I gave up, too, and one day soon after that I met the agent on my way to work.

"Turner," he said, "I was looking at your land on Chalk Hill. Are you not working it?"

"It's no good," I said. "It's hard work for nothing."

"The master was telling me," he went on, "that the men seem to have given up. He says he can manage the Chalk Hill land well enough with his new plough. Will you sell your plot to him?"

Tom and the others talked to me about it. The land was no good to us, we decided. We might as well make a bit of money out of it. "A bit of money" was right. The agent knew the land was no good to us, so he *beat us down*[9] to a few shillings each.

And that was how the men of Littleton lost their last bit of land. They lost their pride as well. From then on they were little better than the slaves of the squire and the big farmers.

3.
Wreckers

There are always people who prefer to lead a life of crime instead of working honestly for a living. In the eighteenth century there was as much crime as there is today. Anyone walking alone in a city at night was likely to be knocked down and robbed. Highwaymen stopped coaches on the roads and robbed travellers of their belongings. At sea, pirates attacked merchant ships and made off with their *cargoes* [10]. And round the shores of Britain there were some particularly unpleasant criminals — the wreckers. Here is the story of one of them.

Down in Cornwall where I was born, there are many sandy *coves* [11] with high cliffs each side of them and lines of rock running out under the water. Many a sailor has met his death on those rocks, and I'm going to tell you all about it.

There was an old man in our village whose name was Reuben. He was deaf and dumb and very old — but he could see all right, and his job was to sit up on the cliffs as night fell and look out to sea. He had an old *spy-glass*, [12] and if he saw a ship heading our way he used to come down to the inn as fast as he could to tell us.

If it was a bright, moonlit night we would stay in the inn. But if it was windy and wild — that was the best time for wrecking. The sailors would be out there, you see, unable to see where they were going, with the wind blowing them off course. They'd all be leaning over the rails, looking for the light from a lighthouse.

Well, we gave them a light to look at. We used to go up to the cliffs, and old Reuben would take a lantern and wave it above his head, cackling all the while. He was a wicked old man.

The sailors would come closer to check the light — and then they would run aground on the rocks.

"Look at that, mates! What a shame!" we used to say, and then we'd rush down to the sandy cove and launch our little boat.

I remember one night — a wild winter's night it was — when we wrecked the *Golden Dawn*. She was a fine ship, bound for London from Africa. When she ran on the rocks, they tore the bottom off her. By the time we rowed out to her, half the crew were dead and most of the others had dived into the water. Not much hope for them, of course — if they didn't hit their heads on the rocks they would have died of shock in the icy sea.

We didn't worry about that, though. You should have seen how quickly we emptied that ship's **holds** [13] and rowed the cargo back to the beach! About three hours' work, and it was all over. Or so I thought.

Our leader, Jack Taylor, rubbed his hands when the last boat-load was brought back.

"That's it then, lads," he said. "These cases will be safe enough here till the morning, and then we can carry them up to the village in our own time."

We'd hidden the packing-cases under an overhanging cliff, and we were feeling pretty pleased with our night's work as we went home. I was walking with Jack and Reuben. The dawn was just coming up when we reached the top of the cliff path and turned down into the village.

Then, out of the corner of my eye, I saw something move. I put my hand on Jack's arm. "Sst," I hissed as quietly as I could, and nodded towards the side of the path.

We stood still and stared. There seemed to be a dark shape there. Perhaps it was a bush, I thought. Fancy that — three tough wreckers scared stiff by a bush!

But it wasn't. As we watched, the dark shape split up into four, and four sailors came out of the shadows and stood on the path in front of us. I heard Jack draw in his breath sharply.

"You fools," he said. "They must have escaped while we were dealing with the cargo."

"That's right, my friend," said the leader of the four. "And while our shipmates were drowning."

He came forward and took a swing at Jack, knocking him to the ground. Another of the sailors came for me and put his arm round my neck.

"I'd like to snap your neck in two," he said in my ear. "My brothers were in the *Golden Dawn* with me. Now they're torn to pieces on the rocks."

For a moment I thought it was the end for me. But the leader of the sailors took charge, and soon had all three of us roped together. They dragged us to the shadow of some bushes, and waited for the rest of our gang.

That day we were taken to Bodmin Jail to wait for our trial. When the day came, Jack and the others were sentenced to death. They were the wickedest set of ruffians, the judge said, that he had ever seen. I don't know why I didn't hang with the others. Perhaps it was because I was only a young lad at the time. Instead I was sent in a prison ship to Australia. But that's another story.

4.
Brighton Camp

In 1793 war broke out between Britain and France, and it went on, with a few short breaks, until 1815. By 1804 a young French army officer called Napoleon Bonaparte had become Emperor of France, and had worked out a plan to invade England.

If you have read Book 5 in this series you will remember that in 1588 the Spanish had a plan to invade England. Since then, no one else had tried. But the news that Bonaparte ("Boney", as everyone in Britain called him) was building a great fleet of invasion *barges* [14] on the French coast caused a great panic. Plans were made for an invasion warning to be sent all over the country if the French ships were sighted. Watchtowers were built on the coasts of Kent and Sussex. A canal was built behind the Kent coastline so that troops could be rushed from their camps to the beaches. Thousands of *volunteers* [15] signed up for the army, and new camps were built to house them. One of these was at Preston Park, near Brighton, but everyone called it "Brighton Camp."

My sister, Sue, and I work at our dad's stall in the fish market at Brighton. When we heard that the Volunteers had come to Brighton

Camp we could hardly wait to go and see them. Our dad heard us whispering about it, and said "Kate! Sue! You're not to go near the camp."

"No, Dad," I said. "No, Dad," said Sue. But that day, when we closed up the stall, we slipped away to Preston Park to see what we could see.

My, what a scene it was! The Volunteers were marching tall and straight, making patterns of lines across the square in their blue and scarlet uniforms, with their muskets gleaming in the sun! I wish I had been able to paint a picture of it. And sometimes, in my mind, I can still hear the sound of the **fife** [16] and drum band, and those good old tunes ringing out in the clear air.

Then the parade ended and the Volunteers were free for the evening. You won't be surprised to hear that Sue and I soon found two lads for ourselves. Mine was called Robert. He said he was twenty-one, but really I think he was only about eighteen. He told me that he came

from a place called Manchester, which he said was a city full of smoky

black chimneys. He was glad to leave Manchester and was planning to be a soldier all his life.

"But first," he said, "I'll have to see how I get on when we fight Boney."

"Are you really going to fight Boney?"

"We must," said Robert. "If we don't, then he will send his army over and become Emperor of England as well as France. And we'll all have to learn to speak French and eat frogs' legs."

"Ugh!" I said. "Don't be disgusting!"

I saw a lot of Robert. Every afternoon, when I could slip away, I used to go to the camp and wait for the parade to be over. Then Robert would come out of the gate, tall and handsome in his uniform, and we'd go for a walk.

Robert used to tell me all sorts of things about the war. He said that the Royal Navy was on patrol in the Channel to make sure that Boney's invasion fleet didn't reach our coast. Another time he told me that Boney had a plan to lure our navy out into the ocean, and then send his army across the Channel quickly while our sailors were out of the way. I longed to tell my dad all these stories, but of course I couldn't, because then he would know I'd been with the soldiers.

Then, one day, something terrible happened. I was walking around Brighton with Robert, and Sue was with her soldier, and I was beginning to think that, at last, Robert was going to ask me to marry him. We were in one of those narrow streets in Brighton called The Lanes, and Robert and I were in front.

"The trouble with being a soldier," said Robert," is that a soldier can't really get married. He never knows when he might have to go off and fight."

"I wouldn't mind that," I said. "Think of all the tales you'd have to tell when you came back."

I've always thought that the next thing he would have said would be to ask me to marry him. But he didn't get the chance. Because suddenly, there in front of us in the narrow street, I saw my dad. When he saw Sue and me and our soldier boys, his face went white with anger.

"Kate! Sue!" he shouted. "What did I tell you?"

And he rushed forward, snatched us away and hustled us back up the street.

We struggled and pleaded with him, but it was no good. My dad was furious because we had disobeyed him, and he was sure that his daughters were too good to marry soldiers. If only he had met Robert, he might have changed his mind — but it was too late now.

My dad kept a close watch on us after that, and made sure we went straight home every day after we closed up the stall. It was about a couple of weeks before I could find an excuse to go down to Preston Park. I said I was going to deliver some fish to an old lady I knew down that way.

I knew something was wrong long before I reached the camp. There was no sound of marching feet, or fife and **tabor** [17], or muskets being drilled. There was just silence. And when I got to the camp the square was empty. There was not a single soldier in sight.

But there was just one old man poking about where the tents had been, probably looking to see if anything useful had been left behind. I ran over to him.

"Where are the Volunteers?" I asked.

He straightened his back.

"Oh, they've gone," he said. "Marched out this morning. Gone to Germany, some people say. We won't see them again."

I couldn't help letting the tears roll down my cheeks. The old man put a hand on my arm.

"Here, don't cry," he said. "The camp won't be empty for long. There'll be some more soldiers here soon."

But I knew that it wouldn't be the same. And it never was.

5.
Death of a hero

One of the most famous battles between the French and the British took place at sea in 1805. It was the Battle of Trafalgar, and it was fought in the Atlantic near the southern tip of Spain.

The commander of the British fleet was Admiral Lord Nelson, who had already won many battles against the French. But Trafalgar was to be his last. This true story tells how he died.

In 1805 I was a midshipman, training to be a naval officer, on board Nelson's flagship *Victory*. I was eighteen that year, and had been in the Navy for eight years.

I was the signal midshipman. My job was to take the signals or messages from the signals officer, Lieutenant Pasco, and pass them to John Roome, the signalman. Naval signals used a system of flags, so the signalman had to be quick at sorting out the right flags to send any message that had been ordered. Lieutenant Pasco, John Roome and I had to spend all the long hours of the battle on deck.

Admiral Villeneuve, the French commander, was trying to reach his home waters from Spain. He had twenty-one of his own battleships and twelve Spanish ships under his command. The British fleet numbered twenty-seven.

Lord Nelson's plan was to cut across the path of the French fleet and break it in two. Then the rear half would be destroyed or made helpless before those in front had time to turn and come to the aid of their friends.

As the sun rose on the morning of 21st October, we could see the French fleet in the distance. Lord Nelson went round the *Victory* to check that all was ready for the battle. Then he went below to his cabin, to pray for "a great and glorious victory."

After that, he came up on deck and said that he wished to send a signal to the British fleet. "I wish to say to the fleet," he said, "England **confides that**[18] every man will do his duty."

I heard Lieutenant Pasco say to him, "It will be quicker if you will allow me to say 'England expects' instead of 'England confides that.' It will take less time to spell out with the flags."

Lord Nelson agreed with this, and soon John Roome was hunting out the flags and arranging them ready to hoist.

After that, there was another signal — the order to "**close action**."[19] And we sailed forward to meet Villeneuve's fleet.

As it turned out, I was the first British sailor to be injured in the battle. As we sailed towards the French line, a French cannonball smashed into the upper deck, scattering oak splinters all around. One of these hit my arm and caused a bad wound. But there was no time to send for the doctor, so I bound the wound as best I could and carried on at my post.

That was not the end of my troubles. The *Victory* sailed on and broke through the French line. As we did so, we collided with the French battleship, *Redoubtable*, and a fierce **musket-battle** [20] broke out between their sailors and ours. I was trying to see, through my spyglass, what was happening to the rest of the fleet. As I stood there, a musket-ball hit the metal tube of the glass, smashing it, and another thudded against my body — to be stopped by my heavy watch.

It seemed that the Frenchmen on the *Redoubtable* were determined to kill as many of the *Victory*'s crew as they could, and then board us. Crouching on the decks of the *Redoubtable*, they were above us and could fire down on us more easily than we could aim and fire back.

I seized a musket and joined in the fight. One by one our men fell. Now and again we hit one of the Frenchmen. Then the worst thing of all happened. A french musket-shot caught our Admiral, Lord Nelson, in the back. He cried out, "They have done for me at last, my backbone is shot through!" As he was carried below, we went on firing at the French, more determined than ever now to see every man dead.

Slowly we picked off their men, and they picked off ours, until there was only one man left on the deck of the *Redoubtable* — and only me left on the deck of the *Victory*. The Frenchman tried to escape by climbing the **rigging** [21] under cover of the sails. "He mustn't get away," I thought as I brought the musket to my shoulder. I saw a flash of his clothing among the sails and fired. He fell out of the rigging like a stone, into the water.

I went below to report to Captain Hardy, the *Victory*'s captain, that whoever it was that had shot our Lord Nelson was now dead. But down below there was sad news for me. One of the other officers drew me to one side. "Don't trouble Captain Hardy now," he said quietly. "Lord Nelson has just died of his wounds."

The time was just after four o'clock in the afternoon. Before he died, Nelson had heard that the Battle of Trafalgar had been won for the British. But our hero, Lord Nelson, was dead.

NOTE   This chapter is based on the reminiscences of Cdr. John Pollard RN, 1787–1868, the author's great-great-great-grandfather.

6.
A new world

In 1815 Napoleon was finally beaten at the Battle of Waterloo, and peace returned to Europe. But the world had changed a great deal since 1790. New factories had been built to supply the weapons and uniforms needed in the war. More coal was needed to make the steam to drive the factory machines, so more coal-mines had been opened. Because the French fleet had stopped merchant ships coming into English ports, the British had had to grow more of their food at home, and farmers grew rich.

Suddenly, in 1815, all this came to an end. Soldiers and sailors coming back from the war could not find work. Uniforms and weapons were no longer needed, and some factories had to close down. Now that food could once again be brought from abroad, the price of home-grown crops fell. There was terrible poverty.

Some people blamed the machines in the factories. If it were not for the factory **looms** [22] which could do the work of several people, they said, there would be hand-weaving work for everyone. In some places, unemployed workers broke into factories and smashed the machines. Others blamed the new machines that were working on farms, and gangs of farm workers without jobs broke up the farmers' **threshing-machines** [23]. Often troops were called out to stop these outbreaks of violence, and sometimes the troops opened fire against their own people. People said, "We won the war. Why are our old soldiers and sailors so poor, when they fought for their country and brought us victory?"

There was no answer from the government of the day. But side-by-side with the scandal of the returning soldiers who could not find work there was another scandal — the employment of children as young as six to work in Britain's mines and mills. Many of these children had no parents and had been placed in **orphanages** [24]. No one wanted to pay to look after them — and so when factory owners offered to find them work, to work they had to go, however young or ill they might be. Here is the story of one of them.

My name is Robert. I don't know if that is my real name, because I can't remember my mother or father. Robert was the name they gave to me in the workhouse where I was brought up.

I can't remember much about the workhouse, except that it was run by a cruel, short-tempered man called Mr Hawkins who often beat us if we did the slightest thing wrong. I can just remember, too, some of the food we had there — thin porridge, just water with a few oats in it, and a kind of oatcake biscuit which was sometimes mouldy.

When I was seven, Mr Hawkins called all the children of my age together in the workhouse yard. There was a gentleman coming to see us, he said. If he liked the look of us, he would give us work. Mr Hawkins showed us how to lick the palms of our hands and rub them over our hair to brush it. "The gentleman will be looking for smart boys," he said, "so make yourselves smart!"

The gentleman arrived. He walked up and down the rows of children — girls as well as boys — and sometimes asked us to show him our teeth or bend our arms to show our muscles. If he tapped us on the

shoulder, Mr Hawkins had said, he must go out to the front. The gentleman tapped me on the shoulder.

There were about twenty of us at the front when he had finished. He went over to speak to Mr Hawkins, and I'm sure I saw him pass Mr Hawkins some money. Then we were loaded on to a cart.

It was a slow journey, and the cart was bumpy. Some of the children were sick. At last we came to a tall, black building, with two tall chimneys stretching up towards the sky.

"That's Litton Mill," said the carter. "That's where you're going to work, you poor devils!"

But we didn't stop there. We went on until we reached a long, low building like a barn. It had no windows, only openings in the walls with sacks hung across them. Inside it was dark and smelt damp.

'This is where you sleep," said the carter. "Only don't sleep too late, or the **overseer**,[25] Mr Sharpe, will wake you up with his whip."

He was only too right. The next morning, a bell rang about six o'clock — and not long afterwards Mr Sharpe came in, swinging a long cane. Anyone who was still in bed, or who seemed to be dressing too slowly, caught a stroke or two.

There was a pump outside, but no soap was provided for us. I don't know if you've ever tried to wash in cold water with no soap. It's hopeless. So most of us didn't bother, and just got dirtier and dirtier day after day.

At seven we arrived at the mill. The machinery was already running, and we were shown our places and what we had to do. My job was called "piecing." The mill wove cloth, and sometimes the threads would break. It would have wasted time to stop the machines to pick up the broken ends, and the piecer's job was to climb under the frame of the loom, find the broken ends and tie them together. There wasn't much room to move, and that was why the job was given to small children.

Piecers had to be very careful. They were crawling about in a machine that was running at full speed all the time. If they made a mistake and put an arm in the wrong place, it might be chopped off by part of the machinery. Several of my friends were injured like that. But we had to keep going. To make sure, the factory owner employed "overlookers" who walked up and down the rows of machines to make sure everyone was working. If the overlooker thought you were lazy, he'd give you a kick, or hit you with his stick. Some days, if I was tired and not able to work as hard as I should, I would come back at the end of work covered with bruises.

I stayed at Litton Mill for about four years, I think. Then, one day, the overlooker got drunk and picked on me. He began to chase me round the looms, waving his stick and threatening to kill me. I think he would have done it, too. So I dodged him, ran out of the door, and went back to the lodging-house for my few bits and pieces. An hour later I was walking along the high road on my way to London. What was going to happen to me? I didn't know. All I knew was that I was never going to work at Litton Mill again.

7.
The clearances

Terrible things happened in Britain in the nineteenth century. Some of them — like Robert's story in the previour chapter — took place in the new factory towns. Others happened in country districts. Some of the worst happened in the Highlands of Scotland, where poor people had, for hundreds of years, scraped a living from their plots of land without interference from anyone.

The Highland farmers or crofters knew every inch of their land and what could be grown or raised on it. They were happy people. They were cut off by the mountains from what happened in the rest of Britain, but they had their own language, their own songs and their own stories and wanted only to be left alone to farm their little plots of land, paying their small rents to the landowner.

For most of the Highlanders, their landowner was the Duke of Sutherland. The Sutherlands were a wealthy English family who had come into the land by marriage. In 1801 the Duke of Sutherland earned £300,000, which would have lasted him and his children for the rest of their lives, even if they had never earned another penny. But rich people are sometimes greedy, and it seemed to the Duke of Sutherland that if he got rid of the people on his land and reared sheep instead, he could become even richer. He decided that the people must go. He would arrange for ships to take them overseas, to one of Britain's colonies. There they could start a new life and he would be rid of them.

Betsy MacKay remembers what happened in the year 1816 and tells us about it.

I was fifteen that year. I was the eldest of four children, and had to look after the others while my mother and father worked on the croft and tended our beasts. My grandmother lived with us, and she was old and weak. I had to look after her as well.

If you live in the Highlands, you don't worry much about what might happen next year or the year after that. You think about how fat this year's beasts are getting, and how much they might fetch when you sell them, and whether there's enough food stored away to get through

the winter. So when we heard about the Duke's plan to get us off his land, we didn't take much notice.

Then the Duke sent a **minister** [26] to talk to us about the land across the sea called Canada. The minister told us that if we went there we would have ten times as much land — new land, where beasts would grow fat.

"We want to stay here," we said.

Then, one morning, Mr Sellar came to our house. He was employed by the Duke to make sure that Highlanders left their crofts. There were four or five men with him.

My father and mother had gone out early to drive some cattle to market. I was giving my brother and sisters and my grandmother their breakfast.

"Where is Angus MacKay?" called Mr Sellar.

"Gone to market," I said. "He'll be back at dusk."

"Too late," Mr Sellar said. "You have ten minutes to pack your-selves up and get out of the house. Hurry!"

I didn't know what he meant. The children were screaming, and I tried to calm them down. Mr Sellar sent two of his men into the house and they began to take out our furniture and belongings and set them out on the grass.

I rushed up to one of them and caught hold of his sleeve. "What are you doing?" I yelled. "Leave us alone!"

He shook me off so roughly that I fell down in the mud. I brought the children out and sat them down. "It's all right," I kept saying. "Don't cry like that. Please don't cry. It'll be all right."

Inside our croft, I could hear an argument going on. I went in to see what it was all about. Mr Sellar's two men were trying to move my grandmother. She was saying, "I'm not going! I'm not going!" She sat in her chair, waving her arms at the men whenever they tried to shift her.

Our dog was barking, my brother and sisters were screaming. I went out to see to them, and as I passed Mr Sellar I saw him nod to one of the men. The man reached to his belt, pulled out a torch, lit it, and went up to the thatched roof of our house. The flames licked out from the torch on to the roof, and in a minute it was well alight.

"No!" I screamed. "No! My grandmother's in there!"

"She had her chance to come out," said one of the men. "And she wouldn't. So let her burn, the old witch."

I'm not a brave girl, and if I had had time to think about what I was doing I would probably not have done it. But I dashed in to the house, which was filling with smoke, and found my grandmother sitting in her chair. "You must come!" I said to her. "Now. With me. Take my hand and run."

She sat there without speaking.

"Please!" I shouted at her. "Take my hand and come!"

I grabbed her hand and pulled her up. "Keep your head down!" I told her, and we went as fast as we could through the smoke and flames which licked down from the roof. I could hear her coughing behind me, but I kept hold of her, kept pulling, and kept running.

At last we were out in the air. Both of us collapsed on the ground, breathless. My grandmother was sobbing. I was too frightened to do anything but lie there and take in great gulps of air.

Then I felt something poking me in the back. I rolled over and it was Mr Sellar's stick.

"Tell your father when he comes back," he said, "that he had his chance to go, and chose to stay. Now he must go in any case. He can take you all wherever he wants, as long as it is off the Duke's land."

Then Mr Sellar and his men rode away, to set fire to another house. I sat there for some time, stunned and frightened. Then I asked myself why this had happened to us. We were doing no harm. We had done nothing to anger the Duke or Mr Sellar. But Mr Sellar would have been quite happy to see my grandmother burned to death. Why? Why? Why?

★ ★ ★ ★ ★

The MacKay family were lucky. They went to Oban, sailed for Canada, and started a new life there thousands of miles away from the Duke and Mr Sellar. Betsy's grandmother went with them and was able to enjoy a few years of peace and comfort before she died. But not every family was so lucky, and even today, in the Highlands of Scotland, there is bitterness and anger about what was done to the Highland people nearly two hundred years ago.

29

8.
Building an empire

It was not only criminals, like the young Cornish wrecker we met earlier, and families like the MacKays who were turned out of their homes, who went abroad to start a new life in a new country. There were many other **emigrants:** [27] farm workers out of a job, skilled workers hoping for better wages, shopkeepers, and the younger sons of English landowners. All were hoping for a better life and, although life was hard at first in a new country, many of them succeeded.

There are few families in Britain which do not have distant relatives in the United States of America, Canada, Australia or New Zealand. In the sixty years after 1815, about eight million people emigrated from Britain, about half of them to the United States. Jamie's family went to Australia and he tells his story.

I was about ten when there was great excitement in our house one day. A letter had come from my Uncle Jack in Australia. We had never had a letter from Australia before. I couldn't believe that it had come all the way from Uncle Jack's farm in New South Wales to our house in Wiltshire.

What Uncle Jack said in his letter was even more exciting. He had been in Australia for five years, and now, he said, he was thinking about taking some more land to make his farm bigger. He would need some

more help. He said, Why didn't Dad bring Mum and the children out there? "I know you're not afraid of hard work and there'll be plenty of that," Mum read to us as we sat round the table, "but it will mean a healthy life for the children and work for them as well when they're ready."

"Oh, let's go there! Please!" I said.

"Sh," Mum said. "You father and I will have to think about it. We can't decide now."

Every day for a week I asked Mum if she and Dad had "thought about it yet." Every day she smiled and said that she'd tell us as soon as they had made up their minds. Every night, when we went to sleep, we could hear them in the other room, talking on and on.

Then, one morning, Mum said: "Well, we've decided. We're going."

From then on there was hardly time to think. Dad had to arrange to sell his *livestock*, [28] book our places on the ship, write letters to all the rest of our family, and most important of all, write to Uncle Jack to tell him we were coming. About a month after that we arrived at Bristol to join our ship.

We had a shock when we saw where we would be living for several weeks. Dad had to save as much money as he could for our new home, so we were travelling "steerage." This was the cheapest way to travel. When we got on board, we followed a crowd who were disappearing down a narrow *hatchway* [29] in the deck. We climbed down a steep ladder until we reached a lower deck where rough wooden bunks had been arranged on two levels, with only a narrow space between each

row. Mum and Dad tried to keep us all cheerful, but none of us was looking forward to the voyage.

Since we came to Australia, we've heard tales from other emigrants which show that we were fairly lucky. In bad weather, the hatches were shut and steerage passengers had to stay in their bunks. On some voyages, this happened for days on end. It only happened to us once, and then only for three days. But that was bad enough.

When it was fine we were allowed to go on deck. That was where the cooking was done. Mum had to buy food from the sailors and then wait in line for a turn at one of the stoves. The food was poor and there wasn't enough of it, but we were glad to be up in the fresh air for a while.

We landed at Melbourne in Australia. There had been no time to arrange for Uncle Jack to meet us, so we had to wait in Melbourne until he came to collect us. He arrived on a big farm cart with a kind of canvas tent on top.

We travelled for days until we reached Uncle Jack's place, near a town called **Wagga Wagga**. [30] He had cleared out a barn for us to live in while Dad built us a proper house. That first night, my brother Peter and I lay on our new straw mattresses and watched the night close in outside. Mum and Dad were sitting at a table at the other end of the barn, talking and planning. The night noises were loud and harsh, not at all like those of Wiltshire.

Peter was only six, and he didn't understand what was going on.

"When are we going home?" he asked. "I don't like this place."

"You'll have to start liking it," I whispered. "This *is* home, now."

9.
The iron road

Up to about 1850, few people travelled more than ten miles or so from home in the whole of their lives. Travelling by coach was expensive, and ordinary people did not have horses of their own. Travel was only for the rich or the adventurous.

The railways changed all that — but, strangely enough, the men who built the first railways were not really interested in carrying passengers. Most of a railway's profit would come, they thought, from carrying freight such as coal and bricks.

The first real railway, with trains drawn by steam engines or locomotives, opened between Stockton and Darlington, in the north-east of England, in 1825. At once there was great excitement. Everyone could see that it would be faster and cheaper to carry goods by rail than by road or canal. Plans were made for railways to run all over Britain, and by 1850 almost all the main lines that we have today had been built.

After that, railway building went on more slowly until, by 1900, there were few small towns or even large villages which did not have a railway station of their own.

The railway builders were great engineers. They had to tunnel under hills, make bridges over rivers and valleys, build up embankments and dig cuttings. Building a railway was just as difficult as building a modern motorway — but railway engineers had no modern *equipment*. [31] Most of the work was done by men with shovels, picks and wheelbarrows. Thousands of workmen, called "navvies", found jobs on the railways. Here is the story of one of them.

They call me Paddy because I come from Ireland, but my real name is Patrick. In 1842 I went up to Woodhead, between Sheffield and Manchester, to help with work on the tunnel there. The Sheffield to Manchester line crosses the moors of the Pennines, and at Woodhead it travels under the mountains for over three miles. At that time, it was the longest railway tunnel that had ever been built.

There were always jobs to be had at Woodhead because the work

was so hard that no one could stand it for long. We lived in huts roughly put together with stone, with a roof of turf. It was draughty and dirty — but we didn't care much about that because all we wanted to do when we stopped work was to sleep. We worked all day every day, Sundays as well. The only way to get a day off was to say you were ill — and then you didn't get paid.

The way we worked at Woodhead was this. First the miners went in with explosives. They blasted away the rock and slate. Then, when the rock had stopped falling and the dust had settled, we went in with shovels and barrows and cleared the **rubble**. [32] Sometimes rocks would fall around us while we worked, and one or two of my mates were injured or killed that way. Sometimes if it had been raining, and it rains a lot up there, we would work up to our knees in water. Think of that, hour after hour, day after day — and nowhere to dry your clothes when you got home!

After we had cleared away the rubble, the bricklayers would come in behind us and line the tunnel with bricks, while we moved on to the next section. It was slow work, and it seemed as if it would never end. 35

But it ended for me one day in the winter of 1843. My mate, Tim, and I were working inside the tunnel, clearing away rock that had been blasted down. You could still smell the gunpowder from the blasting, and somewhere up above there was a steady trickle of water from the roof. My shirt was wet through, and the water on the floor of the tunnel was beginning to soak through my boots. Tim was working behind me.

Suddenly, I heard him shout "Look out, Paddy!"

I straightened up, but I was too late. A shower of rocks, dislodged by the trickle of water, came hurtling from the roof and knocked me sideways. One boulder fell across my leg and pinned me to the floor.

It didn't hurt if I kept my leg still, but when I tried to shift the boulder by flexing my muscles there was a sharp pain in my shin.

What was more unpleasant was that I had fallen into a pool of cold, stinking water, and now I was soaked to the skin. My lamp had been knocked away in the rock-fall, and I couldn't see anything except, a long way away, a faint glimmer of light from the end of the tunnel. Then Tim called.

"Paddy! Are you there?"

"Yes," I answered him, "but I can't move. My leg's trapped."

He clambered over the fallen rocks to me. He still had his lamp and he held it up to see how I was. He put the lamp down and tried to shift the boulder. He grunted and strained, but it wouldn't move.

"I'll go and get help," he said. "I won't be long."

"Can you leave me the lamp?" I said.

He found a place to stand it, and went off as fast as he could over the pile of rocks and slate. "It's going to be a long wait," I thought. "It'll take several men to move that rock."

I looked round. The trickle of water was louder and stronger now, and I could see it running down the tunnel wall. Suddenly I discovered something. When I first fell, the upper part of my leg had been out of the water. Now it was covered. I felt down there. The water was covering my knees. It was creeping up my thighs. The water's way out of the pool had been blocked so the level could only rise. It wouldn't be long before the water level reached my waist, and then my chest, and then my shoulders, and then. . .

I tried again to free my leg, but it was no use. I lifted myself up on to my elbow, and then straightened my arm so that my head was a few more inches out of the water. I tried to work out how fast the pool was filling, and how long Tim might take to get back with help. Apart from this worry, the cold of the water seemed to be eating its way into me. I started to tremble, and my teeth were chattering. Perhaps it was partly from cold, partly from fear.

Then I noticed that my pick had fallen fairly close to me. If I
stretched out, I just might be able to reach it. . . Yes, I could. At least
I could touch it. Perhaps if I stretched a bit more. . . Yes, I could get
two fingers to it, three, four. Another heave. I had the handle in my
hand. I pulled, and the pick was mine again.

If I could lever away some of the smaller rocks, I thought, there
would be more room for the water and so the level would rise more
slowly. I started heaving at the rocks, but I could use only one hand on
the pick because I needed the other to hold myself up. I used the pick
like a **battering ram**, [33] stretching out as far as I could and pushing
against the small wall of rock. But I was getting tired and weak from
the cold and, although a few rocks shifted, the water kept on rising.

I stopped to rest, panting with the effort. Then I heard a call.

"Paddy! Hold on, we're coming!"

"Be quick," I yelled. "I'm trapped in the water!"

It seemed to take hours before they arrived, but it must have been
only a few minutes. By now the water was over my ribs and I couldn't
keep still for the cold. As for my legs, I couldn't feel them at all.

Tim came back with two huge Irish lads, and all three were carrying strong iron poles. In no time at all they had levered the rock away from my leg and pulled me out of the pool of water.

I leaned back against the tunnel wall.

"How's your leg?" asked Tim. "Can you feel anything?"

I couldn't — I was still too cold. Tim knelt down and felt my leg with both hands. "I can't feel any break," he said. He began to rub hard, trying to bring the feeling back into it. Slowly I began to feel warmer.

"See if you can stand on it," said Tim.

I tried. It felt stiff and sore and bruised, but there was no real pain. So, leaning on Tim on one side and one of the Irish lads on the other, I made my way slowly back to the tunnel mouth.

There we met Jock, the ganger, and told him what had happened. He looked down at my leg, and then at me. "You'd better take the rest of the day off," he said, "and we'll see you again tomorrow."

"Not me," I said. "I'm never going to work in Woodhead Tunnel again. I'm going up to get my pay."

And I did. I went down south and found work on the Cambridge line. There are no tunnels down there.

10.
The Great Exhibition

In 1837 the eighteen-year-old Princess Victoria became Queen of England, Wales, Scotland and Ireland. It was the second time since Queen Elizabeth that Britain had had a queen as ruler. Victoria did not die until 1901, so she was Queen for almost sixty-four years.

During those years Britain changed a great deal. The most important change was in industry. British engineering was the best in the world, and British-made ships, locomotives, bridges and machinery were wanted everywhere. In Lancashire and Yorkshire, hundreds of mills span and wove cotton and woollen cloth which was sent all over the world. People said that Britain was "the world's workshop."

It was decided to show off how well the British could make things by holding a Great Exhibition in London. A special exhibition hall made of iron and glass was built in Hyde Park, in London. By 1st May 1851 everything was ready, and on that day Queen Victoria toured the Exhibition and declared it open.

People from all over Europe and America came to London for the Exhibition. From all over Britain there were special trains full of visitors. Some days were "shilling days", when you could see the whole Exhibition for 5p. Remember that in those days there were no films, no radio, no television, and most people didn't even see a newspaper. So it was a great thrill for people to travel to London, go round the Exhibition, and see things that they had never seen or heard of before.

Not all the visitors were out to have a good time. As usual when a large number of people gather together, there were some criminals and tricksters among them. This story is about two country girls, Liza and Jane, who went to the Exhibition, and what happened to them.

When I said I wanted to see the Great Exhibition, my mum wouldn't hear of it.

"A girl's not safe on her own in London," she said.

But when I told her that Jane was coming with me, she changed her mind. "Jane's a good, sensible girl," Mum said. "Very well, you can go — as long as you promise to be back on the nine o'clock train."

I don't know which was the most exciting part, deciding what clothes to wear, or getting on the train at the station, or arriving in London for the first time in my life, or seeing the great shining Exhibition Hall in the park! I don't think Jane and I stopped talking for a minute! Of course, we wanted to see everything — the famous Koh–i–Noor diamond, and the statues, and the jewellery — but what we enjoyed most was looking at the other visitors, some of them people from the country like us and others in beautiful fine dresses and the men in tall hats. Some of them were foreigners and we couldn't understand a word they were saying. One of them asked us the way, but all we could do was to stare at him and giggle. He must have thought English people are rude.

After a time I said to Jane, "I must sit down for five minutes. My legs are tired after all this walking." So we went to one of the **refreshment**[34] rooms and had something I'd never seen before. It was called Strawberry Ice.

Well, we were sitting there eating our Strawberry Ices when a young man came up to our table. He was a very well-dressed man, a real gentleman, I thought. He was wearing a tail-coat and smart grey trousers, with a rose in his buttonhole and a tall hat. He took this off as he came up to our table and bowed.

"Ooo-er," I said to Jane.

"I do beg your pardon," he said in ever such a posh voice.

"I wonder if I might have a word with you two young ladies?"

"I don't think we've been introduced," said Jane in her most **snooty**[35] voice.

"I'm sorry," said the young man. "My name is Jack Smith. Whom do I have the honour of **addressing**?"[36] Posh people talk like that all the time, you know.

"I am Miss Jane Swann and this is my friend Miss Liza Jones," said Jane, still snooty.

"I am delighted to make your acquaintance," said Jack.

"We shall have to be going in a moment," said Jane. "Our parents are waiting for us in the main hall," she lied. I almost blurted out "Ooh, Jane, you **fibber**!"[37] but just managed to stop myself in time.

"I was wondering if you could help me," said the young man. "The fact is, I seem to have run out of small change. I've only got a **sovereign**,[38] and the young lady at the counter can't change it. And I do so want a cup of tea. Could you possibly change my sovereign for two halves, or something smaller?"

We started hunting in our purses for small change, and by putting coins on the table managed to make up a sovereign's worth. I collected them all up in my hand (I had my gloves on, of course) and put them into his. With the other hand he fished in his pocket for the sovereign.

"That really is most kind of you," he said. "I am most humbly grateful." But as he was saying this he seemed to see something out of the corner of his eye. He stood up and stared.

"Is that . . . No, surely not, it can't be . . . Her Majesty? Yes, I think it is, **by Jove**!"[39]

He was looking out of the refreshment room into the Exhibition Hall.

Jane jumped up. "The Queen?" she said. "Is it really?"

"I'm almost sure," said Jack. "Come and stand here and see if you can see her."

Jane went over, and of course I followed. We couldn't see any sign of anyone who looked at all like Queen Victoria.

"I can't see her," I said, turning to Jack. But he had gone. There was no sign of him. And he hadn't given us the sovereign.

We looked all round the room, but he was nowhere to be seen.

"He's got our money!" I said.

'We must find a policeman!" said Jane.

"Policeman?" said a man near us. "There's one in the main hall, just by the way out."

The policeman listened to our tale kindly, but when we'd finished he shook his head sadly.

"I'm sorry," he said. "There's nothing I can do. There are a lot of **rogues** [40] like him about in London. You'll never see him again — or your money."

Fortunately we still had our railway tickets home, so it didn't spoil our day out too much. But I didn't dare tell anyone at home how foolish we'd been, and how easily we had been tricked. I'll tell you this, though — since that day I've never trusted anyone with a posh voice.   **43**

11.
A day by the sea

Liza and Jane, like most visitors to the Great Exhibition, travelled to London by train. Rail travel made it possible for ordinary people to enjoy a day in the country, or by the sea. Special trains called "excursions" were run by the railway companies, with very low fares, and the journey itself was a great treat for people who were used to staying at home.

Most British holiday resorts like Blackpool and Brighton became popular in the first years of Queen Victoria's reign. There were special shops and stalls where people from the excursion trains could buy presents to take home or food to eat. For people who stayed longer than one day, hotels and boarding-houses were built. Two years after their trip to the Great Exhibition, Liza and Jane, with their boy-friends Dick and Bob, went to Brighton for the day, and had another adventure.

Of course, we didn't tell Mum that Dick and Bob were going with us. She wouldn't have liked that, because she was always saying that we were too young to go out with boys. At eighteen! Anyway, we arranged for Dick and Bob to meet us at the station where the excursion train was waiting.

That train was crowded! "You'll have to sit on my knee," said Dick.

"Don't you be so cheeky," I said, "or I won't go at all."

We managed to find seats at last. At the station Dick had bought a map that unfolded so that you could read about the sights on the way. It was ever so interesting.

When we arrived at Brighton we went straight down to the sea-front. We watched a ship come in and moor alongside the pier. Someone said it had come all the way from France. Then we went along the beach to look for shells. Jane said she wanted to drink some sea-water.

"What do you want to do that for?" I asked.

"It's good for you, my Mum says," said Jane — but when she had taken a sip she made a face and spat the rest out.

44   "It's *salty*!" she screamed.

"Of course it is," said Bob. "All sea-water's salty."

"Know-all!" said Jane, and splashed water at him.

"Are you going to bathe?" I said to Jane.

"No, I'm not!" she said. "Don't be so disgusting!"

So instead we all weighed ourselves on one of the new weighing-machines, and after that we went to the camera obscura. This is a kind of tent with a tiny hole in the top that the light comes through. There's a white table in the middle, and on it you can see a picture of the beach and sea-front. Outside again we had some fish and chips for our dinner, and followed that with a strawberry ice-cream like Jane and I had at the Great Exhibition two years ago.

Then we all bought funny hats. Dick had a pirate's hat and Bob had a tall hat like a policeman's. Mine was a floppy straw hat like a donkey's, and Jane's was covered with paper flowers.

"We must take care not to miss the train home," said Jane. She always worries about things like that.

"All right," said Dick. "Let's find some small gifts to take home, and then we'll go to the station."

I bought a little white jug for Mum that had "A present from Brighton" printed on it, and a funny clay pipe for Dad, and a stick of rock for my little brother. We all finished buying our presents except for Dick. He said that he was "looking for ideas."

"You'd better start having ideas about how we're going to get home if we miss the train," said Jane. "Bob and I are going back to the station, aren't we, Bob?"

"Come *on*, Dick," I urged him.

"You go on. I'll catch you up," he said.

I was so cross with him. What was the use of going to Brighton with your boy-friend if you had to go back without him? When we walked up West Street to the station I felt that people were looking at me, sorry for me because I hadn't got a boy.

The train was there already, filling up quickly.

"Let's find seats by the window," said Jane, "and then you can wave to show Dick where we are."

Time went by. More people got on. We could hear the engine getting up steam, ready to start.

"Oh, what shall I do?" I said, wringing my hands. "Shall I get off and wait for Dick?"

"Certainly not," said Jane. "That wouldn't do any good. We don't want to leave *two* of you behind."

A railwayman came down the platform slamming all the doors. "Hurry along for the excursion!" he shouted. One or two people rushed down the platform— but Dick wasn't among them.

Then everything seemed to happen at once. The whistle blew and the train gave a **lurch**. [41] I heard someone shout "Hey, you — be careful!" There was a crash as one of the train doors was opened and shut again. And then — there was Dick, red-faced, with his collar all out of place and his hair standing up on end.

"Dick!" I said. The train was moving now, gathering speed as it climbed up the slope out of Brighton station. "What on earth . . . ?"

"I was looking for something special," Dick explained as he tried to get his breath back. "And I found it. Look."

He opened a paper bag, and out of it he pulled a locket on a chain. "Who is that for?" I asked.

"You, of course," said Dick, holding it out.

The locket and chain looked like gold, but of course they were only made of brass with a kind of gold paint on them.

"You nearly lost the train," said Jane sternly. She didn't like it because Bob hadn't bought her anything like that. "And you'll have to stand all the way home, because someone's taken your seat."

"No I won't," said Dick. "I'll have Liza's seat, and she can sit on my knee."

Jane sniffed. But after he'd bought me that lovely present, I couldn't let Dick stand all the way home, could I?

12.
School for everyone

Today every young person in Britain has to go to school from the ages of five to sixteen. And there is a school for everyone to go to.

Until 1881 children went to school only if their parents wanted them to. In any case, there were not enough schools for everyone.

In 1870 the Government decided that it must do more to educate young people so that they could take jobs in factories and offices where skilled workers were needed. The plan was to build a school in every town or village where there wasn't one. Many schools in Britain date from this time, and perhaps you know or may even go to one.

But schools were very different in those days. Harry Wise first went to school in 1885, and this is what he remembered about it when he was an old man.

There were about seventy of us, all in one big room, all ages from the infants to the big boys and girls. There was only one way the teacher could keep us in order, and that was with the stick. We got the stick for almost anything — talking in class, not getting our sums right, even for smiling.

The infants had a teacher of their own — well, she wasn't a real teacher. She was one of the big girls who could read and write well, and she taught the infants their letters. The infants had one end of the room and the rest of us were at the other end. We sat in long rows, and the desks and chairs were fixed together. This meant that if you were small you had to stand up to do any writing, and if you had long legs, like me, you were always cramped and uncomfortable.

Let me tell you about some of our lessons. Every morning, we had spelling. The teacher would write five words up on the blackboard and we had to learn them. We used to sing them out like this — "a-p-p-l-e spells apple", and so on. Then the teacher would wipe the words off and go round the class, asking each one of us a spelling. If you got it wrong — whack!

Then there were sums. The teacher wrote them up on the board and we copied them on to our slates and worked them out. Yes, slates.

Schools didn't use much paper in those days, because it was cheaper to chalk on to slates and wipe it off when the work was over. We used to clean the slates with our sleeves and there was dust everywhere.

If it was a fine day, sometimes we went out into the school yard for drill or what you would now call "P.E.". We had to march up and down like soldiers, and to exercises, keeping time, all together. If you didn't keep time with the others — well, you can guess what happened.

Sometimes the teacher gave us what he called an "object lesson." He would bring something to school, it might be anything — a white mouse in a cage, or a plant, or even something like a coal-shovel — and give us a lesson about it. When he'd finished, he would ask questions round the class. There was trouble for anyone who hadn't listened carefully. But object lessons were so boring that it was hard not to drop off to sleep.

There was always big trouble in our school round about the end of June. Round our village there were a lot of strawberry fields, and when

51

the fruit was ripe the children of the village were needed to help to pick the crop. Our parents needed us to help, too, because there wasn't much money about in those days and they needed the few shillings we could earn at strawberry-picking.

The teacher didn't like it, because his job was to make sure we went to school unless we were ill. Every strawberry-time he used to send for the School Board Man. This was a man who came round to see why children weren't at school.

I remember one year, my father said to me and my brothers: "It's strawberry-picking tomorrow. No school for you."

"We'll get into trouble," I said.

"Don't you worry about that," said my dad. "If the School Board Man comes round, I'll see to him."

So off we went strawberry-picking, and it was a good crop that year. I liked strawberry-picking, because you were allowed to eat any fruit that was too ripe. Well, there we were in the field, and suddenly a head appeared over the hedge. It was Mr Lambert, the School Board Man.

"Why are you boys and girls out here when you should be in school?" he asked, getting out a notebook to write down our names.

"Our dads said," someone said. "Our dads told us."

"I shall have a word with your dads," said Mr Lambert. "Now then, I want all your names."

When he had finished writing them down he snapped his notebook shut.

"Right," he said. "Now, back to school, all of you."

"But . . ." someone argued.

"Don't 'but' me," shouted Mr Lambert. "Off you go!"

We picked up our strawberry baskets and began to *trail* [42] off. But just then my dad came along. "Hey, where are you all going?" he asked.

I didn't know who frightened me most, my dad or the School Board Man.

"He told us to go back to school," I explained, pointing at the School Board Man.

"I'll soon see about that!" said my dad, and he went up to Mr Lambert.

"These are my children and my mates' children," he said, "and they do what I tell them, not what you tell them."

Mr Lambert went red and started to argue. But my dad didn't give him a chance.

"We've got big families to feed and clothe, and if our children can earn a bit of money so much the better," Dad went on. "And if you're not out of sight in two minutes I'm going to carry you down to the station myself and put you on the train!"

The School Board Man hesitated for a minute, and then walked off, muttering to himself. When he was at a safe distance, he shouted: "You'll hear more of this!"

"Right, lads and lasses, back to the strawberries," said Dad.

But the School Board Man was right. One day not long afterwards, a letter came to our house. My dad opened it, and then went white with anger.

"Look at this!" he said. "I've got to go to court. For 'wilfully keeping your children from school,' it says here."

Mum was worried. "We've never had any trouble like this before," she said. "Will they send you to prison? Oh, what are we going to do?"

Dad didn't have to go to prison, though. He went to court, and the **magistrates** [43] **fined** [44] him five shillings (25p). Even so, that was hard, because five shillings was a lot in those days.

He wasn't the only one. Every dad whose children had been in the strawberry field that day had to pay a fine.

My dad went to see the farmer. "Look," he said, "we've all had to pay a fine because our children helped with your strawberries. How would you get them picked if our children didn't come along?"

"You're right," said the farmer. "I'll have to have a word with the School Board."

So next year, when strawberry time came round, the teacher told us that we could have a special week's holiday for picking. We could tell he didn't like it, but he had to do what the School Board told him.

But it wasn't a complete victory for us. The teacher saved the worst bit of news to the end. "To make up for your week off," he said, "school will start a week early next term."

13.
A man's life

All through Queen Victoria's reign, Britain went on building up her Empire. People went out to live in Canada, Australia and New Zealand. In India there was an army of British and Indian soldiers. Some of the islands in the West Indies were ruled by Britain. Smaller islands in the Atlantic and Pacific oceans were taken over to be used as harbours for the ships that travelled to and fro, bringing **raw materials** [45] like wool and cotton to Britain, and taking back goods made in British factories.

A map of the world in those days would look rather strange to us. There were still many parts of the world that had not been explored. A map of Australia, for example, would show towns and villages, mountains and rivers near the coast, but there were huge blank areas inland where no one from the western world had ever been. The same was true of Africa.

Man has always wanted to find out more about the world he lives in. Those unknown, blank areas on the maps were a challenge. Perhaps, people thought, there was gold there. Perhaps there were different **civilizations** [46] that no one had ever heard of. Perhaps there were tribes which could be converted to **Christianity**. [47]

David Livingstone was a Scotsman who was interested in converting Africans to Christianity, and he spent the last thirty years of his life exploring Africa. He was the first white man to see the Victoria Falls,

which he named after the Queen. He died while he was searching for the source of the great River Nile, deep in the heart of Africa.

One of the most famous meetings in history took place between David Livingstone and an American newspaper reporter, Henry Morton Stanley. Stanley, too, became an explorer, but by accident. This is the true story of how it happened.

My name wasn't always Henry Morton Stanley. I was born in Wales and spent my childhood in a workhouse. I was given the name John Rowlands.

I hated workhouse life. The food was poor and there was not enough of it. The beds were hard. We had to do wretched, back-breaking work. There were two ways for a young lad to get away from the workhouse. One was to join the army. The other was to run away to sea.

I ran away to sea and became a cabin-boy on the Atlantic ships. That was a hard life too. So one day, when we were docked at an American port, I slipped away and found a job in a **warehouse**. [48]

The owner of the warehouse, Mr Stanley, took a liking to me and adopted me as his own son. His full name was Henry Morton Stanley, and that was the new name he gave me. Mr Stanley brought me up, saw that I was educated properly and arranged for me to become a citizen of the United States.

Then war broke out between the northern and southern states, and I became a soldier. After that I took a job as a newspaper reporter, and because of my knowledge of wars I was sent to Europe and Africa to write stories about the fighting there.

Then I was given a new job by my paper, the *New York Herald*. This was what I had to do. The British explorer and missionary, David Livingstone, had been missing in Africa for three years. No one knew where he was, or whether he was alive or dead, but many people feared that he must have been killed, or had died from disease. The *New York Herald* said that it would pay for me to find Livingstone.

In 1871 I set out on my journey. It would be hard for you to imagine what it was like to set out into an unknown country. We knew that Africa was full of wild animals. Many explorers had been killed by them, and Livingstone himself had been badly wounded by a lion on an earlier exploration. There was danger, too, from tribesmen who did not want the white man to explore their country. There was always a risk of dying of some tropical disease. And as well as all that, explorers could easily simply lose themselves and wander round until the animals or disease or the hot sun finished them off.

I gathered together a large party for my expedition. We took enough stores to last us for a long journey, and I made sure that the Africans in the party knew the country well.

It was a long and terrible journey. We knew the direction in which Livingstone had gone, but we knew very little more. We had to trace his steps by asking tribesmen if they had seen a white man pass that way some time before. On we went, and I became less and less hopeful that we would find him alive — or that we would find him at all.

We had been travelling for eight months through East Africa when, on 10th November 1871, we came to a village called Ujiji on the shores of Lake Tanganyika. As we approached the village, there was great excitement among the huts, and from one of them an old man stepped out to look at us. I screwed up my eyes against the sun to see who it was. But my servant, Selim, recognized the man first.

"I see the Doctor, sir!" he cried. "What an old man! He has a white beard!"

As we came closer I saw that the man had grey whiskers and a moustache, and was wearing a faded blue cap, a red shirt and grey tweed trousers. I wondered how to greet him.

I walked up to him, took off my hat, and said, "Doctor Livingstone, I *presume*?"[49]

"Yes," he said, smiling and raising his cap.

"I thank God, Doctor, that I have found you," I said, clasping his hands.

I stayed with him for several weeks, and we did some exploring together. But then it was time for me to return. When we said goodbye, I could not help the tears coming to my eyes.

Livingstone waved from his doorway until we were out of sight. He died about a year later, from fever. I was the last white man he ever saw.

14.
Working lives

If you could go back in time one hundred years, you would not believe your eyes when you saw the kind of lives that most working people lived.

Their homes were cramped, dirty and overcrowded. If they had meat to eat once or twice a week, they thought themselves lucky. Most of the time they lived on food like bread, potatoes and suet puddings — food that fills you up but does not contain enough **protein** [50] to keep you healthy. They worked twelve hours a day or more. If they fell ill, there was no pay. The factories were noisy and dirty, and often dangerous as well. Smoke from factory chimneys filled the air of the cities. Wages were low. For most people, there was no hope that things would improve.

Some workers joined trade unions to try to bring about better wages and working conditions. But if an employer found that his workers had joined a union, there was nothing to stop him sacking them. This is what happened in a match factory in London in 1888, and the story is told by Emmy, who was there.

There weren't many jobs round our way for girls who left school, but if you couldn't find any other work you could always go to the match factory.

It was a terrible place. There were no "safety matches" in those days, and match-heads were made of phosphorus. The job of the match-girls was to dip matches into the phosphorus. Then the matches were packed into boxes that were made outside the factory by people working in their own homes.

I don't suppose you have ever smelt phosphorus but, believe me, it's a terrible smell. Worse than that, it gives off fumes, and the fumes can give you a disease called "phossy jaw." When it starts, "phossy jaw" feels like toothache, but it gets worse and worse until the whole of your jaw is aching. There is no cure for it, and in the end your jaw jams tight and won't move.

You might say, how on earth could the match company find people to work in their factories? Or, why couldn't matches be made in some other way? The answer is that no one would work there if there were any other jobs to be found. And there *were* other ways of making matches, but they cost more.

So there we were, in 1888, working for twopence an hour at a job that might one day **cripple** [51] or kill us. And that wasn't all. Although we worked with such dangerous stuff, there was nowhere in the factory where we could wash our hands. We had to carry trays of matchboxes on our heads from one part of the factory to another, and in time this made us go bald. If we were late, or if we were caught talking or singing — not that we had much to sing about — we were fined by our employers. When the company decided to put up a statue of the Prime

Minister, it decided to help to pay for it out of our wages — without even asking us!

That year, there was a terrible row at the factory. A newspaper printed an article about "phossy jaw" and what it was like to work at the match factory. Our employers were very upset, and wanted us to sign a letter saying that we were well-treated. "No," we said. Outside the gates we had a meeting of all the girls, and the lady who had written the article came to talk to us.

'There's only one way to deal with this," she said. "You must all **strike** [52]"

'Strike?" we said.

"Yes. Say you won't work unless wages go up and conditions in the factory are made better."

"But how will we live, if we don't go to work?"

"I can help you," said the lady.

So we told our employers that we were going on strike, and, as we had expected, they sacked us all. "When you find out how hard it is to live without money, you'll soon be asking for your jobs back," they said.

But the lady writer did as she had promised, and helped us. She wrote more articles about us, and when they appeared in her paper readers sent money to help us in our fight. There were meetings about our strike, and at the end of every meeting a hat went round for money.

The strike went on for two weeks. In the end our employers had to give way. They put up our wages, improved conditions in the factory, and agreed to look for other ways of making matches without using yellow phosphorus. And that was how the match-girls of East London won a place in the history books.

NOTE   A few years later, the use of yellow phosphorus for match-making was banned by law.

15.
Ideas at work

The people of the nineteenth century were great inventors, and their ideas made great changes in the lives of everyone between 1800 and 1900. You have already read about the railways. Another great change was at sea where, by 1900, sailing ships like Nelson's *Victory*, made of wood, had been replaced by steel steamships.

But everyday things changed, too. Gas pipes were laid so that homes, factories, offices and the streets could be lit by gas. By 1900 some towns already had electric power stations. Joseph Swan and Thomas Edison invented the electric light bulb. In America, Alexander Graham Bell invented the telephone. Photography, sound recording and the petrol engine were other nineteenth-century discoveries.

There were some very strange inventions, too. One man invented a model railway that could be laid from the kitchen to the dining-room table to carry in hot food and take away the dirty dishes! Another designed a kind of head-harness to stop people snoring.

Among all these inventions, some of the most useful may not seem, at first, to be very important. One was the **interior-sprung mattress**, [53] first made in 1871. Before that, people slept on mattresses made of horse-hair or even straw, which were dirty and lumpy. Thousands slept better once they had bought an interior-sprung bed. Another idea that changed people's lives was the sewing-machine, which Isaac Singer invented in America in 1851. Before that all clothes had to be sewn by hand. Sewing by machine made clothes cheaper and easier to make, and enabled more people to wear the latest fashions.

The problem that many inventors worked on was to work out a way of "horseless transport" on the roads. The steam-engine idea had been used for road vehicles, but road locomotives, or traction engines as we call them now, were slow, heavy and clumsy, and used large amounts of coal and water. No one would want to go for a Sunday-afternoon drive in a traction engine! In Germany, Britain, France and America, engineers were working on ideas for petrol-driven cars. The petrol engine had already been invented, but the engines built so far were not powerful enough to drive a car full of passengers.

The first engineer to build a successful car was a German, Karl Benz. In 1885 he took his first drive through the streets of Mannheim,

where he lived. But there was still a lot of work to be done before cars were to take the place of horses and carriages. Cars still broke down too often. Sometimes they even blew up! Passengers often had to get out and push when they came to a hill, and sometimes, going down the other side, they had to cling on for dear life when the brakes failed! To drive a car in those days, you had to be a very keen motorist.

Gradually, however, cars were improved. Engines became more reliable, and it was a great step forward when a Belfast vet, John Boyd Dunlop, invented the pneumatic (air-filled) tyre. Before that, tyres were made of solid rubber and, as there were very few smooth, level roads, a car ride was a very bumpy experience. No wonder some cars were called "boneshakers" or "rattle-traps."

Two engineers who joined forces to build cars were Mr Rolls and Mr Royce. Here is Henry Royce's story.

My father died when I was nine, and when that happened in Victorian times it meant very hard times for the rest of the family. To try to bring some money in, I took on any job I could find, such as selling papers and delivering telegrams. Then, after a while, I got a job as an **apprentice** [54] at a railway works, and that was where I started to learn about engineering.

In those days you had to pay to be an apprentice, in return for being taught your trade. For seven years my mother would have to pay out money and get nothing back. She couldn't keep up the payments and so I had to leave the railway works. We were both sorry, but there was nothing else to be done.

Well, I took a few jobs here and there, learning more about engineering, and then I decided to start up on my own. I set up in business in Manchester, with a small engineering workshop where I took on any work that was going. By never turning a job down, and by working long hours every day of the week, I built up quite a successful little business.

At that time every engineering business was having a go at making cars. You didn't need a huge factory then. Every car was built by hand. You could make one, sell it, and then start on the next. I built my first car in 1903.

It was a good car. Some people just rushed ahead and made any old kind of car as long as it would go. But I'd waited until I'd got everything just right.

It was about this time that I first met Charles Rolls. He wasn't a working man like me. His family was rich, and he was really only interested in motoring as a hobby. But he had a garage business and was looking for a new car to sell.

We got on well from the start. Charles Rolls knew how to sell cars, and I knew how to make them. By 1906 we were making so many that we needed a larger place to work, and so we moved from Manchester to Derby. In the same year we went down to the London Motor Show, and took with us our newest, best car yet — the Rolls-Royce Silver Ghost. "The best car in the world", we called it.

The orders came flooding in, and Rolls-Royce became a successful partnership. Sadly, Charles Rolls didn't live to enjoy his success, because four years later he was killed while enjoying another of his hobbies — flying. But the company lived on.

16.
Taking to the air

On 17th December 1903, on a patch of barren sandy heath in North Carolina, a man called Orville Wright did something that man had been wanting to do for centuries. It was the first powered flight. Men had flown before in baskets slung under balloons, but this was the first aeroplane flight, and the first using engine-power.

Orville Wright's aircraft, which he had built with his brother Wilbur, bumped along the sand-dunes and at last took off. It skimmed across the heath for a few yards, and then landed.

Strangely enough, very little notice was taken of this. The local papers in North Carolina reported it, but America's national newspapers took little interest. The Wright brothers could not find anyone in America interested in their invention, so they set off for Europe to try their luck there.

In Europe there was a great deal of interest in flying, and soon engineers were trying to make their own aircraft. In England, the owner of the *Daily Mail* offered a prize of £1000 to the first pilot to fly across the English Channel from France to England.

It's only about twenty miles from Calais, in France, to Dover, and today no one would get very excited about a flight of that length. But no one had done it before. All previous flights had been over land, and the pilots used roads or railway lines to guide them. Aircraft had no radio or other aids to *navigation*. [55] Pilots had no parachutes, and they flew too close to the earth for parachutes to work, in any case. Aircraft engines coughed and spluttered as if, at any moment, they might just stop and plunge machine and pilot to earth.

On 25th July 1909, Louis Blériot, a Frenchman, set out from a field near Calais to try to win the £1000 prize. Early in the morning, just after dawn, he took off for England. The French Government had ordered a *destroyer* [56] to follow his course by sea, in case he had to be rescued from the water. Meanwhile, on the cliffs near Dover, a crowd of people had gathered to see Blériot arrive. In the crowd was fourteen-year-old David Brown who tells us of his experiences.

The *Daily Mail* had told us that Louis Blériot was going to try to cross the Channel that day, if the weather was fair. So that morning I got up early, before it was light, and walked all the way from Dover to Shakespeare Cliff above the town. There were plenty of other people on the road, and once or twice motor cars full of passengers passed us. There was a strange excitement in the air. People talked quietly. I think we all felt that something important was going to happen.

When we arrived on the cliff, we found that many people had got up even earlier than we had done. Some had come all the way from London. A tent had been put up for the reporters from the *Daily Mail*. There were policemen standing about, and soldiers from Dover camp. Outside another tent was a hand-cart with a *stretcher* [57] on it.

"What's that for?" I asked a man standing nearby.

"In case there's an accident," he said grimly.

The last darkness of the night went from the sky, and the sun came up across the sea. We turned away from it and peered towards the south. Across the Channel we could just pick out the line of the French coast. Had he started yet, we wondered?

Suddenly there was a shout of excitement from the reporters' tent. "What is it?" we asked each other, and then we heard, passed from one person to another, that a message had come that Blériot had taken off successfully and had been seen heading out to sea, towards England.

After that we didn't take our eyes off the sky, but we could see nothing. There was a haze over the sea, and it began to thicken into

real cloud. Now what would happen? The papers said that Blériot wasn't even carrying a **compass**. [58] How would he find the way? Would he go round and round in circles until he ran out of petrol?

No one spoke. We were all thinking hard, and listening. Somewhere along the Dover road, there was the sound of a motor-car engine. We held our breath for a second. Was it Blériot's plane? "No, it's only a car," someone said, and we all breathed again.

Then there was another sound, faint at first but gradually getting louder. "It's him!" we all shouted. "Listen!" Then, through an opening in the cloud, we saw Blériot's little **monoplane** [59], looking as frail as if it were made of paper. He swooped low overhead and turned to land. The wind caught the aircraft and tossed it to one side. Blériot pulled it straight again and came in, lower. . . . At the last minute the wind caught him again, throwing him off course.

"Stand back! Stand back!" shouted the police and soldiers, making a chain of their arms to stop us all rushing forward.

Down Blériot came again. This time he stayed on course. The wheels brushed the grass. At that moment, Blériot switched off his engine, and the plane bumped along the turf until, with all of us holding our breath again, it stopped.

We saw police and soldiers rush up to see that he was all right. Two Frenchmen followed, and helped Blériot from the **cockpit**. [60] They kissed him on both cheeks. The rest of us shook hands with each other. At the time I thought: "This is silly. It's as if we were **congratulating** [61] each other. But we've got nothing to be pleased about."

But afterwards I changed my mind. We *did* have something to be pleased about. That day, a little bit of history had been made, and we were there to see it happen.

17.
A night out

In the days before radio and television were invented, people either had to make their own entertainment at home or go out to find it.

Most people who could afford it had a piano at home, and playing the piano and singing were favourite ways of spending an evening. This was all right if you were lucky enough to have a pleasant home to live in, with enough room for everyone. But most working people liked to get out of their homes as often as they could. One of the places they liked to go to was the music-hall. There it was warm, unlike home. It was brightly-lit, unlike home. There were good songs and good jokes, and for a while you could forget your troubles.

There were music-halls in most towns, and in London and other big cities there were dozens. The variety shows they put on had something for everybody — comic turns, sentimental love-songs, jugglers and acrobats, even circus acts. The audience could join in the songs, and everyone had a good time. It was a cheap night out.

In our story Edward is taking his girl-friend Lucy to a music-hall in Clapham, South London.

I waited for Lucy at the tram-stop, but when the **tram** 62 stopped and people got off I didn't recognize her at first. Then this tall, lovely-looking girl said, "Hallo, Edward." For a moment I just stared at her.

"My, you look good enough to eat!" I said. She was wearing a new straw hat with flowers and bows on it, and a white blouse and skirt with more flowers. Under her hat, a fringe came down over her forehead. I had my Sunday suit on, but when I saw Lucy I wished I'd asked Mum to give it an extra press last night.

Lucy took my arm. "Where are we going?" she said.

"It's a special treat," I said. "We're going to the Grand Hall. Marie Lloyd's on tonight."

"Marie Lloyd? They say she's ever so good."

Have *you* heard of Marie Lloyd? I'd better explain. When I was a young man, she was one of the most famous people in England. She was a music-hall singer, and so many people wanted to see her that she often sang at three or four music-halls on the same night, rushing from one to the other in her own carriage. Every one knew Marie's songs, such as *A Little of What You Fancy Does You Good* and *Oh, Mr Porter.* You'd hear people whistling them in the street any day.

But now I was worrying about how much money I had in my pocket. At that time I was working in a grocer's shop and didn't have a lot of money to spare. I'd planned to take Lucy to the Grand Hall, in the sixpenny seats, and then I thought we'd have a pint of beer for me and a half for her in the interval, and perhaps some fish and chips afterwards, and then take her home on the tram. That would have cost me about half-a-crown — 12½p to you.

Seeing Lucy dressed up like that, I had to change my mind quickly. I couldn't take her into the sixpenny seats with all the roughs — I'd have to pay ninepence each at least, or maybe even a shilling. And I couldn't ask a girl dressed like a lady to drink beer in the interval. And when we came out, I couldn't expect her to walk along the road eating fish and chips.

It was the first time I'd been out with Lucy. She worked in the next shop to mine, in the High Road. Of course it was a dress shop, so she could probably buy dress materials cheaply and make them up at home. I hadn't thought of that.

Anyway it was too late to worry now. We'd have a good night out, even if I had to walk to work for a week, and go without my meals at mid-day to make up for it.

We went to the shilling seats. You get a good view of the stage from there, and don't have to strain to hear what the comics are saying.

We'd heard all the jokes before, but that didn't stop us laughing. They were jokes like this. The first man says "I say, I say, I say. Have you ever heard of a kangaroo?" And the second man says, "Of course

73

I've heard of a kangaroo," and then the first man says "Well, have you ever heard of a dangeroo?" The second man says "Of course not, there's no such thing as a dangeroo", and then the first man says "Well, you go up to the zoo and you'll find a cage there, and on the outside of the cage there's a notice saying 'These animals are dangeroos.' " He meant *dangerous*, see? Lucy laughed so much at that one that I thought she was going to choke.

Then there was a magician, but he wasn't very good because you could see how his tricks worked, and then some dancers and acrobats. A man came on in a striped blazer, carrying a cane, like one of the toffs you see in the Park, and he sang a few songs. Soon it was the interval. Lucy decided to have an orange drink — thank goodness. Orange drinks are even cheaper than beer.

When we went back to our seats, there were more acts. Some of them were not very good, and everyone was impatient by this time for Marie Lloyd to arrive. At last, almost at the end of the show, there was a hush and a roll of drums. Some of the lights went out, leaving just a small pool of light in the middle of the stage. Everyone was staring at the light.

Then Marie came in. The **audience** [63] went wild. Some of them cheered, the rest of us clapped, and several people in the cheapest seats up in the gallery called out "Hallo, Marie" and "Hallo, duck!" She just stood and waved at them.

The strange thing was that she was quite an ordinary-looking woman. You could hardly have noticed her if you passed her in the street. The band struck up, she started to sing, and it was only then that you understood why she was so famous.

Some music-hall singers sing about things that ordinary people don't know about, such as moonlight in Paris or going hunting and that kind of thing. But Marie sang songs with stories that we all knew about. One of them, *Don't Dilly Dally on the Way*, was about a family moving house piling all their furniture on an old hand-cart. *Oh, Mr Porter* was about a girl on a train who missed her station and was taken on to another one. Of course everyone joined in the choruses, and Marie conducted as we sang.

"That was a lovely show," said Lucy when we came out.

I thought, so it should be, for a shilling each. But of course I kept that to myself.

"What about a fish supper?" I said.

Lucy frowned. "I don't eat in the street," she said.

"No, of course not. I meant a sit-down fish supper. There's a place just round the corner."

If I'm going to take you out again, I thought, I'd better start looking for a better job. But I kept quiet about that, too.

Two ninepenny fish suppers, twopence each on the tram to take Lucy home, and the whole evening had cost me nearly five shillings, double what I'd expected!

At Lucy's gate, I said, "Can I see you again?"

"I expect so," she said.

It was a fine summer's night, so I decided to save twopence and walk home instead of catching the tram. It was a good thing I did, because there were going to be many more nights out with Lucy before we got married two years later.

18.
Workhouse

For people like Edward and Lucy, young and fit and with jobs, life was better than it had been for their parents. They had a little more money to spend, better food to eat, and more treats like nights out or a day's picnic in the country.

The twentieth century had begun. Queen Victoria had died, and her son Edward VII was king. Britain was a rich country, with her factories sending British-made goods all over the world. Some of the worst slums in the big cities were being pulled down and replaced by new flats and houses.

But for some people, things remained as bad as ever. If you were too ill to work, or too old, or if your father or mother had run away from home, or if you were an orphan with no mother or father still alive, there was only one place to go — to the workhouse.

If you have read the earlier books in this series you will remember that looking after poor people has always been a problem. No one wanted to pay for their food or for somewhere for them to live. In 1834 the Government thought that it had found the answer. It decided to build workhouses all over the country where poor people could go. While they were there, they would have to work, keeping the place clean or doing *laundry* [64] or working in the workhouse gardens. And one of the big rules in workhouses was that they must not be too comfortable, or people would want to stay.

Workhouses were terrible places and many people spent their lives in fear of being sent to one. They were little better than prisons. The food was awful, usually bread and thin soup, and people were so crowded that it was difficult to keep the place clean. Colds and coughs spread quickly. The workhouse rooms — wards, they were called — were never warm enough in winter, and in summer they were hot and stuffy.

In the outside world life slowly became better. Inside the workhouse, it was no better in 1900 than it had been in 1834.

Most of the people in workhouses were poor or old or ill. But some of them had just had bad luck. Here is the story of Jack, who went to a workhouse in 1900.

I was a painter, and a good one, too. I started learning the trade when I was twelve, mixing paints and carrying ladders and cleaning brushes. Then my boss let me start painting places that weren't important, like inside cupboards and under staircases. You have to take care when you're painting, and I was always a careful sort of chap. So as I got better at the job I was given better work to do, and soon I was painting all the best rooms in the houses we worked on. When I was twenty I married my wife, Mary, and two years later we had our boy, Peter.

It was about five years after that that I had my accident. My employer at that time was a mean old man who always tried to save money on a job. He would tell us to use two coats of paint instead of three, and to thin the paint down so that it would go further. He was mean about tools and equipment, too.

I'd told him that we needed a new set of ladders: "They're all right," he said. "They'll last a bit longer yet."

The day it happened, I was painting the outside of some windows over the shops in the High Street. It was a fine morning, and I was whistling to myself as I put on the finishing coat of paint. I'd done a really good job, and I was pleased with myself. Suddenly there was a crack, the ladder gave way underneath me, and I was on the pavement, screwing up my face with pain, with my leg bent underneath me.

I was in hospital for several weeks. Mary had to borrow money to buy food for Peter and herself, and then she had to take in washing to try to make a living. When I came out of hospital, I had a bad limp.

"Sorry, Jack," said my boss when I went to see him. "There's no job for a painter with only one good leg."

I tried, but I couldn't find a job anywhere. Then Mary fell ill and couldn't work. Winter was coming, and we had no money to buy coal.

"There's only one thing we can do," I said one night.

"Not the workhouse!" said Mary.

"It's the only place we can go," I said.

I thought my heart would break when we set off for the workhouse a few days later. We had sold our furniture to pay our debts, and all we had in the world were the clothes we were wearing and a little bundle we each carried. When we arrived, we were met by the master of the workhouse. He wrote down our names and asked us if we had had any diseases. A nurse came in and looked at our hair to see if it was clean. Then Mary was sent off to the women's ward, Peter was sent off to the children's, and I went to the men's. I was shown my bed — a plank bed with a thin straw mattress on it and two filthy blankets.

"What's it like here?" I asked the man in the next bed. He spat on the floor.

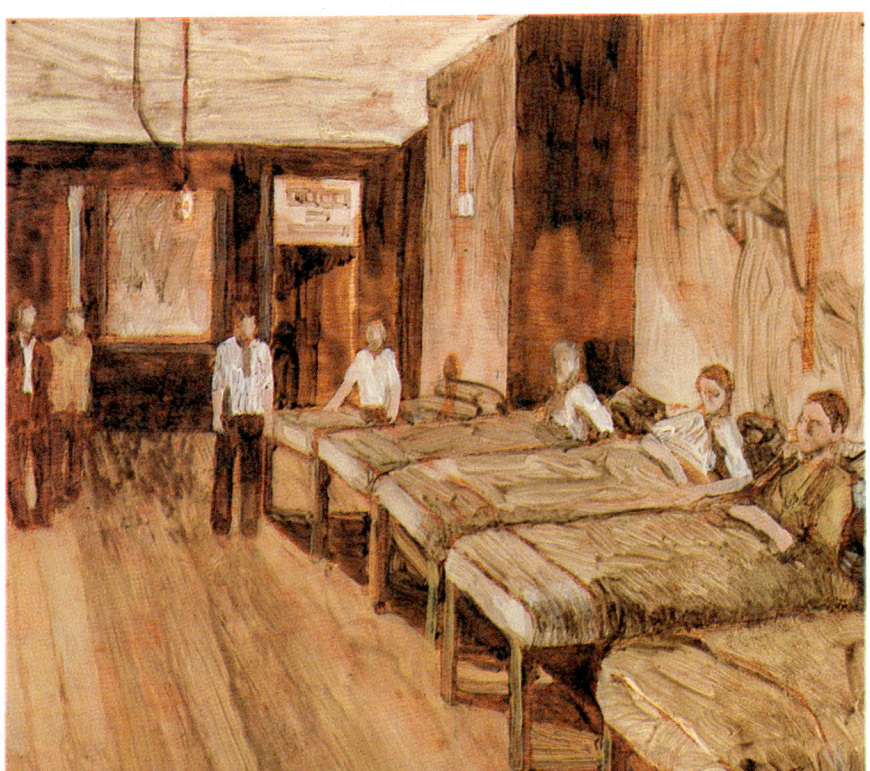

"Terrible," he said. "You get *skilly* — that's a kind of porridge with bits of meat in it if you're lucky — for dinner, dried fish on Fridays, and on Sunday afternoon they let you see your wife and children for an hour or so, if you behave yourself."

"What do you do the rest of the time?" I asked him.

He laughed, and then coughed. "I shouldn't have laughed," he said. "There's not much to laugh about in here. I expect they'll put you on stone-breaking. They show you a big pile of rocks and give you a pick, and you have to break the rocks up into smaller pieces for road-mending. Or they might put you oakum-picking. That's separating the strands of old rope. I don't know which is worse. Stone-breaking breaks your back. Oakum tears the skin off your hands."

He seemed a hopeless sort of chap, and I soon found that everyone was the same. They had given up hope completely. They couldn't see how they would ever get out of the workhouse, and they had nothing to look forward to.

I was given the job of oakum-picking, because with my poor leg I couldn't manage a pick. The ends of the strands of rope are sharp, and they get into your skin and give you a rash. After a week my hands looked as if they'd been boiled.

On Sunday afternoon we were taken to the hall of the workhouse to see our families. When Mary came in and saw me, she burst into tears, and Peter did the same. We were too upset to speak. We just clung to each other and sobbed.

At last I said "What shall we do? What *can* we do?", and Mary shook her head and sobbed, "I don't know. I wish I was dead."

One day soon after that, an interesting thing happened when we were having our dinner of skilly. A visitor came round — I think he was a Member of Parliament — with the workhouse master. At meal-times we went to one end of the dining-hall and collected our bowl of skilly and a piece of bread, and sat down at one of the long tables to eat it. I found a place near the serving-tables. I had just sat down when the master and his visitor came in.

"And this is the dining-hall," said the master. "You can see, sir, that the men are enjoying a good meal at the end of the day."

They went over to the saucepans of skilly. the visitor picked up a ladle, dipped it into the skilly and inspected it closely, sniffing.

"I wouldn't call this a good meal, Mr Stone," said the visitor. "I certainly wouldn't want to eat it."

"We buy the finest oatmeal," said the workhouse master, "and there's beef in it, too. Best beef."

"Then," said the visitor, holding out the ladle to the master, "you will enjoy tasting it yourself."

The master took a step back. "Oh no," he said. "I have eaten my supper already. The food is not for me, but it's good enough for those who are hungry."

The visitor put the ladle back in the pan. "I shall make a report about this, Mr Stone," he said. "This food is not fit to eat, and you know it."

After that the food was a little better for a while, but not much. Every week when I saw Mary and Peter, they looked more pale and ill than the last time I'd seen them. Mary said I looked ill, too. My hands had swollen up, and they hurt all the time. I asked the master if I could see a doctor.

"Doctor?" he said. "I know what the doctor will say. He'll say you're afraid of a bit of hard work, like everyone else in the workhouse."

But he arranged for me to see the doctor on his next visit. It turned out that I had met the doctor before. He had worked in the hospital when I was there after my accident.

Doctor Thorne looked at my hands and wrote out a prescription for an ointment for me to use. Then he looked up into my eyes.

"I've treated you before, haven't I?" he said.

"Yes, doctor," I said, "in the hospital."

"That's right," he remembered. "You broke your leg."

I told him how we had come to the workhouse because there was no work I could do outside.

"You shouldn't be in here," he said. "Surely there's some job you could do."

"If there is, I couldn't find it," I said.

"Let me think about it for a day or two," he said. "I might be able to help."

A few days later, he came back to the workhouse and sent for me.

"You're a painter, aren't you?" he said.

"Yes, sir, and a good one."

"If you could sit down to work, you could still paint, couldn't you?"

"Yes, sir."

"Then I've found a job for you. A friend of mine has started a small toy-making business — doll's houses, rocking-horses, and so on. Could you paint those?"

"Of course I could."

And so it was that shortly afterwards, Mary, Peter and I walked out of the workhouse. The pay in the toy workshop wasn't very good, but it was just enough for us to live on. We found a little house nearby so that I wouldn't have too far to walk. Soon Peter and Mary looked less pale and thin, and we all began to laugh and joke again. Our stay in the workhouse had been like a nightmare — but at last it was over.

19.
Looking back

On 3rd May 1912, Sally Jenkins was 100 years old. She lived in Norwich, and a reporter from the local paper went to talk to her. The reporter asked Mrs Jenkins to look back over her long life and try to remember as much as she could. This is what she told him.

I shouldn't think anyone has ever seen changes as I've known in my lifetime. When I was a girl, London seemed like the other end of the world. Now you can get there in a few hours by train. In the old days it took days, weeks sometimes, to hear what was going on in the world. Now, if something happens in the world today, you can read about it in tomorrow's paper. And nearly everyone can read, too. My dad was the only man round here who could read, and people used to bring their letters and papers for him to read aloud to them.

There are all sorts of changes, wherever you look. There used to be a big cattle fair near here, you know, at St Faith's. They brought the cattle down by road all the way from Scotland — as many as 40,000

some years. Then they fattened them up on the marshes round here and took them on to London. Turkeys, too. They walked to London as well. Now, of course, they all go by train.

Another thing. We're only about eighteen miles (30 km) from the sea here. But I didn't see the sea until I was about fifty years old. Before the trains came, if poor people wanted to go anywhere, they had to walk. So we never went very far. Nowadays people can go to the seaside whenever they want, just for the day or even an afternoon.

To show you how things have changed, I'm going to tell you about when I got married. That was in 1834, and I was twenty-two years old.

Tom and I went out together for seven years before we got married. Seven years! He had to save up, you see. He worked on a farm, and the farmer said he'd let him have a little cottage, but we had to save up for furniture and blankets and so on.

Then, one day, Tom said. "I'm getting fed up with drying my own boots and washing my own shirts. We'd better get married."

"All right," I said. "I've been a long time waiting for you to ask me, Tom Jenkins."

"Right," he said. "I'll go and see the vicar."

The farmer said he'd let Tom have half a day off to get married and wouldn't stop him any pay. That was good of him — most farmers wouldn't have paid him for that half-day. So at two o'clock one Saturday afternoon Tom turned up at my house with one of the farm carts. He'd swept it out and wiped it down a bit, so it was fairly clean. And off we all went to the church.

Honeymoon? [65] No, we didn't have any honeymoon. After the wedding we went to our new house and started putting it to rights. The day after that, the harvest started, so I didn't see much of Tom for a week or two. He was out of the house as soon as it was light, and didn't come back again till dusk. I took him some bread and cheese and a jug of beer at dinner-time, but that was all I saw of him.

I was in service — you know, a servant — at the Hall before I got married, but of course I had to give that up. Tom didn't earn enough to keep both of us, or the babies when they came along, so I had to do gang-work. Do you know what that is? There was a whole gang of us, women and girls and young boys too, and we would go round doing whatever jobs the farmers wanted done, weeding or fruit-picking or anything like that. It was terribly hard work, too, especially in bad weather with the mud coming over your boots and rain soaking into your clothes. The gang-master used to cheat us, too. He would settle on a price with the farmer and keep most of the money for himself. But we couldn't argue. We needed any money we could get, and that was that. When I had young babies, I used to take them with me and let them sleep in a corner of the field while I worked. I couldn't afford not to work.

Now there was another young woman on the gang with me. Her name was Emma, and she had a husband called Jake. A big man, Jake was, **with a short temper**. [66] One day, when the gangmaster paid us, he gave us a shilling **short** [67] because he said we hadn't worked hard enough. Emma must have gone home and told Jake.

The next morning, when we got to work, Jake came along too. When the gangmaster arrived, Jake called out to him.

"Hey, you!" he said. "Are you Mr Edwards?"

"That's right," said the gangmaster.

"I want a word with you, Mr. Edwards," said Jake.

"What's the trouble?"

Jake held out his hand. In it were a few coins.

"This is the trouble," he said. "You're not paying the right money for the job."

"That's as much as I can pay," said Mr Edwards.

"Take your coat off, and we'll find out," said Jake.

They took their coats off and squared up to each other. Of course all the gang gathered round to see what would happen.

Jake hit out first. He caught Mr Edwards just in front of his ear, and this made him wild. He charged at Jake like a bull, with his head down.

Jake was a big man, but he was light on his toes, and he could dance out of Mr Edward's way. Mr Edwards ate and drank too much and he moved much more slowly.

Mr Edwards shouted with rage, turned, and flailed at Jake with both fists. Jake just laughed. It seemed that the other man couldn't hurt him at all.

"Come on, Jake," we all yelled. "Thump him! Make his nose bleed! Knock his teeth out! Knock him down!"

Mr Edwards was panting for breath by now, but Jake was still dancing round him, landing a blow every so often. We loved every minute of it. We'd had more than enough of Mr Edwards and his mean ways.

Then Mr Edwards did a silly thing. Jake liked a fair fight, and he would probably have given him one or two more clouts and then let him go. But Mr Edwards reached out behind him and grabbed a stick from the hedge. It was a heavy fencing stick. He started to wave it round his head. Emma screamed. The rest of us held our breath.

"Try that, would you?" yelled Jake, and he reached up and caught the stick as Mr Edwards swung it. We saw Jake stagger as he caught it in his hand, but he held on. But Mr Edwards let go, and the next moment he was sprawling on the ground.

Jake tossed the stick away. He jumped on Mr Edwards and held him down.

"What shall we do with him, girls?" he said, looking up at us.

"Make him give us our money," I called out.

Jake put his hand in Mr Edward's pocket and pulled out a purse. There were several sovereigns in it, and a lot of small change as well.

"Look at that," said Jake, holding the purse up. "And here's a man who wants to cheat his gang out of their shillings!"

"Let's share it out," suggested one of the girls.

"No, that's no good," said Jake. "That would be stealing, and we'd all go to prison. No, I'll take a shilling for each of you, and leave the purse here for him to pick up later."

Mr Edwards was still struggling, so Jake threw Emma the purse so that she could share out her shillings. Then Jake said, "What shall we do with him now?"

"Put him in the pond," someone suggested.

"Good idea! Come on, Jake!" we all shouted. Jake took his shoulders, and two of the girls took a leg each, and we marched the gangmaster down to the pond.

He made a good splash when we threw him in. And, do you know, he always paid us a fair wage after that.

20.
The end of a world

Looking back in 1912, Sally Jenkins could see many great changes. But the greatest change of all was only two years away. In 1914 war broke out in Europe, and the world was never quite the same again.

For years Germany, France and Britain had been building up their armies and navies. They all wanted to increase their empires. Each of them was jealous of the other. Several times after 1900, war almost broke out. In 1914 it came at last.

In Britain everyone was pleased at first. It was time, they said, to teach the Germans a lesson about which country ruled the world. Thousands of men who had boring jobs and wanted some adventure signed up for the army. At first no one *had* to fight. All the soldiers were volunteers. Everyone thought that the war would soon be over. The British and French would defeat the Germans, and that would be that. "It'll be over by Christmas," the newspapers said. But it wasn't. Four Christmases went by before there was peace again, and by that time millions had been killed and millions more wounded.

In 1914 Guardsman Bert Weston of the Grenadier Guards was 28. He had been in the army for two years. His home was in London, and he was married with a three-year-old son, Francis. He was a machine-gunner.

In the war of 1914–18, over 19 million people died. Guardsman Weston was just one of them. His letters home tell the story of the last months of his life.

Woolwich, 4th August 1914

Dear Louise,

Well, it looks as if things have started. Last night we were having a drink in the canteen when the order came to be ready for action. All day today we have been getting ready to move and checking all our stores.

There is a story that we will be going to France soon. But don't worry about me. They say the war will be over by Christmas, so we can look forward to being together again then.

Your loving
Bert.

France, 6th September 1914

Dearest Louise,

We have arrived in France at last, all ready to have a go at the Germans. All the lads are fighting fit, and that means me as well. Thank you for the parcel of cigarettes. I have sent you a present of French lace in a separate parcel. Look after yourselves, and get ready for me to come round the corner.

Your loving husband
Bert.

France, 9th October 1914

Dearest Louise and Francis,

A special letter for your birthday, Louise. Many happy returns of the day. Let's hope that next year I'll be able to spend it with you. Kiss Francis for me.

We have moved up towards the German lines, and they say a big battle is coming. But we're ready for them. We have been digging *trenches* [68] where we can shelter while we wait for the German troops. They're a bit muddy — the trenches I mean, not the Germans — but not too bad. I expect that, by the time I write again, I will have a good story of victory to tell you.

All my love to you both,

Bert.

France, 18th October 1914

Dear Mrs Weston,
I am sorry to tell you that Guardsman Weston, A., was killed in action yesterday on the Western Front. His machine-gun position was attacked by a party of German troops and he died instantly, with no pain. I am sorry to have to tell you this news, but you will be glad to know that Guardsman Weston died, as he had lived, a brave soldier.
Yours sincerely,
Officer commanding. [69]

The following week Mrs Weston went to the Post Office to collect her first widow's **pension** [70] — five shillings a week.

The meaning of words

[1] *Empire*	A group of countries owned or governed by another country
[2] *settlements*	Small villages
[3] *squire*	Landowner
[4] *agent*	A squire's business manager
[5] *Bill*	A plan to be discussed in Parliament. If a Bill is passed, it becomes an Act of Parliament.
[6] *enclosed*	Fenced off for the landowner's use
[7] *drills*	Machines for planting seeds
[8] *fertile*	Rich, good for growing plants
[9] *beat us down*	Offered us a lower price
[10] *cargoes*	Goods carried by merchant ships
[11] *coves*	Small bays
[12] *spy-glass*	Telescope
[13] *holds*	Places on a ship where cargo is carried
[14] *barges*	Flat-bottomed boats which are towed by ships under power
[15] *volunteers*	People who choose to do something
[16] *fife*	Small flute which plays high notes
[17] *tabor*	Small drum
[18] *confides that*	Is sure that
[19] *close action*	Move into battle
[20] *musket*	Gun with long barrel which fires balls of lead
[21] *rigging*	Ropes which hold up the sails of a ship
[22] *looms*	Machines for weaving cloth
[23] *threshing-machines*	Machines for beating the grain out of ears of corn
[24] *orphanages*	Homes for children who have no parents living
[25] *overseer*	Man in charge
[26] *minister*	Clergyman or parson
[27] *emigrants*	People who go from one country to live in another
[28] *livestock*	Farm animals
[29] *hatchway*	Opening with a door that can be closed down like a lid
[30] **Wagga Wagga**	Say "Wogga Wogga"
[31] *equipment*	Machinery
[32] *rubble*	Pieces of rock and earth
[33] *battering-ram*	Weapon of war that was used to break down the walls of a town or castle
[34] *refreshment*	Food and drink

[35] *snooty*	Stuck-up and unfriendly
[36] *addressing*	Speaking to
[37] *fibber*	One who tells lies
[38] *sovereign*	Small gold coin worth £1.00
[39] *by Jove!*	A saying that means that the speaker is surprised
[40] *rogues*	Villains
[41] *lurch*	A sudden movement to one side
[42] *trail*	Wander, one behind the other
[43] *magistrates*	People who hear cases in court and decide on punishment
[44] *fined*	Made him pay
[45] *raw materials*	Goods which are made into finished clothes or other things
[46] *civilizations*	Groups of people with their own ideas and customs
[47] *Christianity*	Belief in God and Jesus Christ
[48] *warehouse*	Building where goods are stored
[49] *presume*	Believe
[50] *protein*	Food that gives you strength
[51] *cripple*	Injure for life
[52] *strike*	Stop work
[53] *interior-sprung mattress*	Mattress with metal springs coiled inside them
[54] *apprentice*	Young learner of a trade
[55] *navigation*	Finding your way
[56] *destroyer*	Fairly small, fast, armed naval ship
[57] *stretcher*	A kind of bed for carrying an injured person
[58] *compass*	Instrument for showing in which direction you are going
[59] *monoplane*	Aircraft with one set of wings
[60] *cockpit*	Part of an aircraft where the pilot sits
[61] *congratulating*	Exchanging greetings of happiness at success
[62] *tram*	Road vehicle with an electric motor which took power from overhead lines and ran on rails set in the roadway
[63] *audience*	People listening and watching the show
[64] *laundry*	Washing and ironing clothes and bedclothes
[65] *honeymoon*	Holiday after a wedding
[66] *with a short temper*	Easily becoming angry
[68] *trenches*	Ditches
[69] *Officer commanding*	Officer in charge of a unit of soldiers
[70] *pension*	Payment to take the place of wages

When did it happen?

1783	American War of Independence ended. British rule in the American states ended
1789	Start of the French Revolution
1793	Outbreak of war between Britain and France
1805	Battle of Trafalgar
1815	Battle of Waterloo. War between Britain and France ended
1816–54	Highland clearances
1819	Factory Act: Children under 9 must not work in cotton mills. Children of 9 to 16 must not work more than 12 hours a day.
1825	Stockton and Darlington Railway opened
1834	New Poor Law: nation-wide workhouse building plan began
1837	William IV died and Victoria became queen
1839–45	Woodhead Tunnel built
1851	The Great Exhibition in Hyde Park, London Isaac Singer invented the sewing-machine
1870	Education Act: School for everyone who wanted to go
1871	Stanley and Livingstone met in Africa
1875	Alexander Graham Bell invented the telephone
1877	Thomas Alva Edison invented the phonograph (early type of record-player)
1879	Edison invented the electric light bulb
1881	Education Act: Children *must* go to school
1885	First drive by Karl Benz's car
1888	London matchgirls' strike John Boyd Dunlop invented the pneumatic (air-filled) tyre
1901	Queen Victoria died and Edward VII became king
1903	Wright brothers' first powered flight Henry Royce built his first car
1906	Rolls-Royce Silver Ghost shown in London
1909	Louis Blériot's flight across the English Channel
1914	War broke out between Britain and Germany